FORGED ON FREEDOM
THE MAKING OF AMERICA

Roots of the
REVOLUTION

Tammy Gagne

PURPLE TOAD
PUBLISHING

P.O. Box 631
Kennett Square, Pennsylvania 19348
www.purpletoadpublishing.com

FORGED ON FREEDOM
THE MAKING OF AMERICA

The Amendments to the Constitution
The Constitution: Defender of Freedom
The Revolutionary War: The War for Freedom
Roots of the Revolution

Printing 1 2 3 4 5 6 7 8 9

Publisher's Cataloging-in-Publication Data
Gagne, Tammy
   Roots of the Revolution / Tammy Gagne
      p. cm.—(Forged on freedom)
Includes bibliographic references and index.
ISBN: 978-1-62469-066-2 (library bound)
1. United States – History—Revolution, 1775-1783—
Juvenile literature.   I. Title.
 E208.G34 2013
 973.3—dc23
                                                    2013946335

eBook ISBN: 9781624690679

Printed by Lake Book Manufacturing, Chicago, IL

CONTENTS

1 Fighting Together, SPLITTING APART

The American Revolution was the war that won the American colonists their independence from England. Many people mistakenly think of the American Revolution as the first war that was fought on American soil. The truth is that several other colonial wars came before it. One of them, the French and Indian War, marked the beginning of conflict between the colonists and England.

The French and Indian War lasted seven years. In addition to involving England and its British colonies in America, this world war also included the armies of Austria, France, Prussia, Scotland, Sweden, and Wales. Overseas, the war was named the Seven Years War because it lasted from 1756 to 1763. Austria, France, and Sweden were allies in this war. Their main goal was to overthrow Frederick the Great, the rising King of Prussia.

At the same time, both England and France had established colonies in North America, the Caribbean, and India. Both England and France wanted their own colonies to be the largest and most powerful in all three of these areas. France had expanded into the Ohio River Valley in North America. This caused conflict between

With the help of a young colonel named George Washington, the British won the French and Indian War (1754–1763). The French would later become an ally of Washington and the thirteen colonies in the American Revolution.

the French and the colony of Virginia, which had already claimed control of the area.

From 1754 to 1755, the French armies had defeated three different commanders of the Virginia militia. These men included a young lieutenant colonel named George Washington, British Major General Edward Braddock, and Governor William Shirley of Massachusetts. At first, it seemed that Washington might be successful. On May 28, 1754, his men had killed or captured all but one member of a French scouting party. When it became apparent that Washington and his men were outnumbered, they tried retreating. The French soon surrounded them, though, forcing them to give up their prisoners. Washington had done as well as possible with the army he had, but it simply proved to be too small.

The following year Braddock was put in command. He fared much worse than Washington had. In July, Braddock was just a few miles away

British Major General Edward Braddock had 1,400 soldiers in place in Pennsylvania. Even though the British soldiers outnumbered the Ottawa and Potawatamie Indians, the Brits were defeated when the 650 Indians ambushed them.

from capturing Fort Duquesne in the area that is now Pittsburgh, Pennsylvania. The spot was considered one of the most important French positions in the area. Before Braddock's men arrived at the fort, however, they were surprised by a group of French and Indian forces who had hidden in the woods.

Indian scouts had shared intelligence with the British forces, but Braddock refused to listen to it. He knew very little about Indian warfare, and wasn't interested in learning any more about it. He thought that the Indians were inferior and wouldn't deal with them. This proved to be Braddock's downfall. Even though the French and Indian army was outnumbered by a ratio of more than 4 to 1, they defeated Braddock's men swiftly. More than three quarters of his troops of 1,400 men were either killed or wounded at the hands of the French and Indian soldiers.[1] Braddock himself died from a wound he received during the battle.

Later that year, Governor Robert Dinwiddie placed Washington in charge once again. He was named colonel and commander of all Virginia militia forces. Washington was just 23 years old at the time, but he rose to the challenge. One of his duties was to defend the entire 350-mile frontier. The Virginia militia now consisted of 1,000 men, but this was still a small number for such a huge task.[2] Washington managed to hold onto the border, though. In 1758, he and his men finished the task of capturing Fort Duquesne.

England won the French and Indian War, but the victory came at a very high price. Both King George II and his grandson King George III (who came into power in 1760) had borrowed money from other countries to pay for the war. Doing so had placed England deep in debt. Once the war was over, Parliament needed to find a way to pay back this money. The English government also wanted to make the East India Company, a large trade business, successful again. The easiest way to accomplish both of these goals was to tax the colonists on goods delivered to them from this company.

The New England colonies were thriving in the years following the French and Indian War. Massachusetts, New Hampshire, Rhode Island,

One of the most abundant natural resources in the British colonies was timber. The colonists used trees to construct items as large as ships and as small as barrels for shipping British goods. England saw these items as a source of income through new taxes.

and Connecticut were covered with dense forests. The colonists used the abundant timber to produce ships and barrels for transporting British goods. The waters off the New England coast were filled with cod. The colonists caught these fish so England could feed them to their slave laborers in India. Because of these and similar industries, the cities of Boston, Massachusetts, and Newport, Rhode Island, had become busy ports. King George III saw these ports—and the items passing through them—as a means of bringing the colonies' wealth to England.

For more than 30 years, the Molasses Act had been in place in the colonies. This law created a tax of a sixpence per gallon on all sugar and molasses imported from anywhere except England and its territories. The tax was so high that following the law could have put many rum makers in the colonies out of business. For this reason many distilleries worked around the law. Some bribed customs officials to ignore the tax. Others simply smuggled molasses and sugar into the colonies. Since the law wasn't strictly enforced, though, few people got into trouble for avoiding the taxes.

On April 5, 1764, Parliament decided to replace the Molasses Act with the Sugar Act. This new set of laws did three things. The first was to cut the amount of tax on molasses and sugar in half. The British government wasn't being generous, though. Parliament had merely decreased the amount of the tax to distract the colonists from its larger goal. They would now be enforcing the tax more strictly.

The second thing the Sugar Act did was expand the type of items that would be taxed. The Molasses Act created taxes on molasses and sugar only. The passing of the Sugar Act meant colonists now had to pay taxes on items such as coffee, wine, and textiles.

Third, both imports and exports would also be watched more closely now. Colonial businesses that shipped items like lumber and iron would need to fill out lengthy bonding paperwork. The colonists also had to ship these items to England, even if they were to be sent to other European ports afterwards. All of these new rules gave England more control over trade. England would also require suspected smugglers to be tried before judges. Before the Sugar Act, very few smugglers were caught. The ones who were caught were tried by juries. Since the jurors were fellow colonists, they were much more likely to find the smugglers innocent of the charges.

Just four days after Parliament issued the Sugar Act, the government issued the Currency Act. This new law decreased the value of paper money that the colonists used. This act had already been issued to the New England colonies in 1751, but it was now being extended to the other colonies as well. The new law also stated that no further paper currency could be issued. The money that was already in use would be done away with after a certain amount of time.

Sugar plantation owners in the Caribbean sold their sugar products to the British, who then sold it to the colonists in North America. Following the French and Indian War, the Brits taxed the colonists heavily for sugar, molasses, and many other items.

The colonists were not pleased by either the Sugar Act or the Currency Act. Both moves would make life in the colonies harder on the people. Some colonists responded in writing. A Boston lawyer named James Otis wrote a pamphlet titled *The Rights of the British Colonies Asserted and Proved*.[3] In it he stated that taxing the colonists without giving them representation in Parliament was illegal. Another colonist recorded his protest in a petition to the New York General Assembly to the House of Commons. He too, questioned the right of the government to tax the colonists without their consent. Otis and many others felt strongly that the colonists should have a voice in their government. These opinions brought about a phrase that would be repeated by historians for centuries to come—no taxation without representation!

The Treaty of Paris

The end of the French and Indian War came with the Treaty of Paris in 1763. This document awarded all French territory in North America to England and Spain. England took Quebec and the Ohio River Valley. Spain was given the port of New Orleans as well as the land west of the Mississippi River. This was in exchange for its help as an ally in the war.

The end of the war also had an effect on the way the colonies viewed each other. After fighting alongside each other against the French, the colonists had bonded in an important way. Before this time there had been a fair amount of rivalry between the thirteen colonies. Now they had seen what they could accomplish when they worked together.

Map of the colonies after the treaty

HUDSON'S BAY COMPANY

Gulf of St. Lawrence

Louisbourg

Lake Superior

Quebec

Montreal

(MASS.)

Port Royal

(VIRGINIA)

Lake Huron

Lake Michigan

L. Ontario

St. Lawrence R.

N.H.

NEW YORK

Boston

(VIRGINIA AND MASS.)

Lake Erie

Albany

R.I.

MASS.

(VIRGINIA AND CONN.)

PENN.

CONN.

(VIRGINIA)

Philadelphia

New York

N.J.

MD. DEL.

ATLANTIC OCEAN

SPANISH LOUISIANA

Ohio R.

VANDALIA

VIRGINIA

TRANSYLVANIA

Mississippi R.

NORTH CAROLINA

SOUTH CAROLINA

GEORGIA

Charleston

(CLAIMED BY SPAIN AND GEORGIA)

Gulf of Mexico

0   150   300 miles
0   150   300 kilometers

Boundaries after Treaty of Paris, 1763
- British trading company
- British colonies
- Spain
- Quebec in 1763
- Quebec in 1774
- Proclamation Line of 1763
- State boundaries including western claims
- Proposed western colonies

50°N

40°N

90°W

80°W

70°W

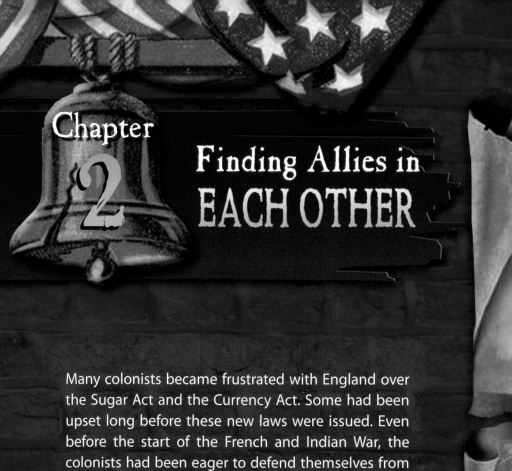

Chapter 2

Finding Allies in EACH OTHER

Many colonists became frustrated with England over the Sugar Act and the Currency Act. Some had been upset long before these new laws were issued. Even before the start of the French and Indian War, the colonists had been eager to defend themselves from the French. They had asked King George I for permission to raise money for this purpose. He refused, however, because he was suspicious of the intentions of the colonial governments.

When the war began, the colonists wanted to do their part. They felt that volunteering for military service was their duty as Englishmen, but the English officers did not view the colonists as equals. When colonists offered to fight alongside the English officers, the English sent many of them away. The English soldiers were more than willing, however, to take colonists' horses, food, and wagons. They even demanded it. When England won the war, the English officers took full credit for the victory, even though many of the colonists did indeed fight in the battles.

King George I refused to let the colonists raise money to help pay for the French and Indian War. He didn't trust the motives of the colonial governments.

Chapter 2

Now England was expecting the colonies to take on the burden of its debt from the war.

The Sugar Act was only the first of many new taxes that England would begin charging the colonists. On March 22, 1765, Parliament passed the Stamp Act. Although its name makes some people think it involved postage for letters, this new law actually had to do with paper. Under the Stamp Act, all official paperwork in the colonies had to be printed on special, stamped paper. Legal documents such as deeds, diplomas, and wills required stamps, as did reading material, such as almanacs, newspapers, and pamphlets. Even advertisements and playing cards had to be printed on this paper that the colonists had to buy from England. And, of course, the stamped paper was sold at a higher cost than regular paper.

By this time the colonists were fed up with new taxes. They also weren't being given the representation in Parliament that they felt they deserved. The Stamp Act wouldn't go into effect until that November, though, so the colonists had some time to consider how they should respond. Some of the merchants had responded to the Sugar Act by boycotting molasses and sugar. The colonists decided that another boycott was in order for dealing with the Stamp Act.

Mobs of angry colonists protested the Stamp Act. They even threatened the customs officers whom England had appointed to distribute the stamped paper. By the time paper shipments arrived in the colonies, almost no one was willing to enforce the act. The date on which the Stamp Act was to go into effect came and went with no major changes to the way business was done. Lawyers and courts used the same unstamped paper for their documents as they always had. Newspapers also continued to use regular paper for their printing.

The newspapers used their businesses to spread their message. They urged other colonists to remain strong in opposing the act. This caused many people to start considering whether England had too much authority over the colonists. Many men responded by writing letters and pamphlets that voiced their own opinions on the matter.

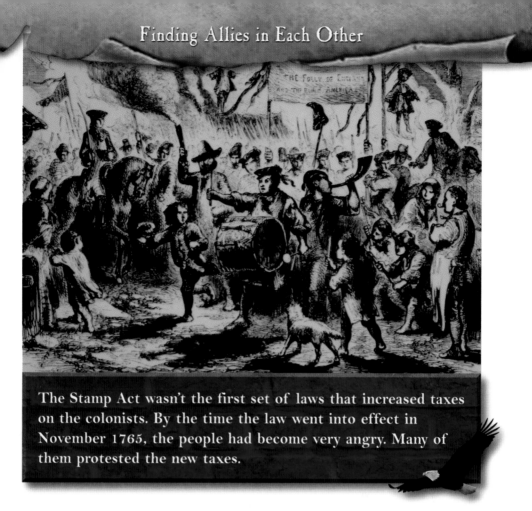

The Stamp Act wasn't the first set of laws that increased taxes on the colonists. By the time the law went into effect in November 1765, the people had become very angry. Many of them protested the new taxes.

Not everyone who spoke out supported the colonists, however. As the member of Parliament who had drafted the Stamp Act, Thomas Whately insisted that England was in the right. He penned a pamphlet called *The Regulations Lately Made Concerning the Colonies and the Taxes Imposed Upon Them Considered* in reaction to the colonists' protests.[1] In this work, Whately argued that the colonists *did* have representation in Parliament. He explained that while they didn't have actual representatives, they had "virtual" representatives. He stated that these Parliament members were looking out for the colonists' best interests as well as the best interests of England as a whole.

Whately didn't think it mattered whether these representatives for the colonies were elected by the colonists themselves or not. In fact, he pointed out that many people in England weren't able to elect members to Parliament. He also explained that England's laws had to be created for the "greater good" of the country. He added that these laws didn't always fulfill the wishes of everyone. The colonists, however, didn't see the problem as an issue of their wishes, but rather their rights.

The colonists immediately rejected the idea of "virtual representation." They didn't think that any representative could be trusted to look out for the best interests of a group to which he didn't belong. They insisted that representatives who had to abide by the laws that they had helped to create would serve the people much better than ones who lived on a different continent.

Like the Sugar Act, the Stamp Act stated that violators would be tried by judges, not juries. The violators would also be required to travel to courts in Halifax, Nova Scotia. For more than 150 years, the colonists had their own courts. The judges were appointed by elected members of the colonial legislatures. The colonists worried that these changes marked the beginning of the end for their court systems. It certainly appeared that England was trying to replace these local courts with their own judges.

Daniel Dulany was among those who supported the outraged colonists. A wealthy lawyer, Dulany was a member of the Governor's Council at the time. His pamphlet, *Considerations on the Propriety of Imposing Taxes in the British Colonies,* was one of the most widely read pieces about the Stamp Act.[2] In it he explained that England should in fact have complete control over the colonies, except in the area of taxes. He argued that when it came to this issue, the colonists should have representatives to speak for them in Parliament. He also made it clear that he disagreed with Whately's concept of virtual representation.

Not only did Dulany's pamphlet circulate throughout the colonies, but it also made its way to England. Several British statesmen who supported the colonists' rights referred to Dulany's words when stating their cases to Parliament. One of the men who quoted Dulany's work was William Pitt, the biggest opponent of the Stamp Act among members of Parliament.

In October 1765, people from several colonies assembled in New York to form the Stamp Act Congress. The people knew that no single colony could get through to Parliament, but together they just might be heard. At first, it seemed that the group wouldn't be able to accomplish much at all. In the beginning, the members couldn't even work together without arguing. A representative from New Jersey became so angry that he walked out even before the proceedings were finished.

The colonists were not going to accept the Stamp Act without a fight. In October of 1765, people from several colonies formed the Stamp Act Congress in New York. They hoped that together they could prevent Parliament from passing the new law.

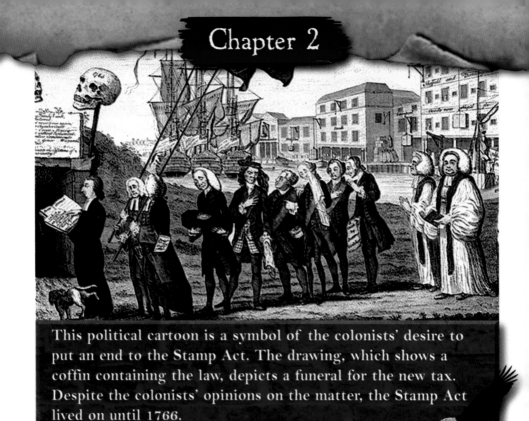

This political cartoon is a symbol of the colonists' desire to put an end to the Stamp Act. The drawing, which shows a coffin containing the law, depicts a funeral for the new tax. Despite the colonists' opinions on the matter, the Stamp Act lived on until 1766.

Only nine colonies sent delegates. No representatives were sent from Georgia, New Hampshire, North Carolina, or Virginia. The delegates that did make the trip disagreed over the amount of control Parliament should have over the colonies. A few of the representatives thought that England shouldn't have been making any laws for the colonies. Most of them, however, simply disputed Parliament's right to tax the people without representation. In the end, the Stamp Act Congress created the Stamp Act Resolves. This document, which was signed by all but one of the delegates, outlined the colonists' belief that they should only be taxed by a government that allowed them representation.

The Stamp Act Resolves did little in the short term to stop the taxation. They did accomplish something very important, however. Up until this point, there was very little interaction between the colonies. Now, even with some challenges, they had managed to come together to discuss the problems they were all facing at the hands of Parliament. Without this unity, they would never be able to face the challenges that lay ahead.

Salutary Neglect

For a long time, the colonists actually enjoyed freedoms that citizens in England did not. The British government tended to rule the colonies by salutary neglect.[3] This concept meant that the colonies were left to take care of themselves. They established their own legislative assemblies, they oversaw their own trade, and they made changes as they became necessary. All of this happened without any major involvement from their mother country.

England used this method of ruling the American colonies to make life at home easier. In many ways, the colonists were governing themselves. This left Parliament free to deal with what it saw as more important political matters on the mainland.

Salutary neglect made some parts of life harder for the colonists. It also came with benefits, though, for both the colonies and England. As the colonists began to trade more with other countries, they made more money. They then spent much of this money on British goods. England also benefited from the raw materials that the colonies were able to produce for them. It seemed like everyone was winning, at least for a while.

Many people think that salutary neglect had a major effect on the separation of England and the American colonies. Because the colonies developed so much on their own, they were more able to pull away from their mother country and stand on their own. If they hadn't been so independent for so long, the colonies might not have resisted the unjust taxes that England was imposing on them so strongly.

Cutting timber in the New York colony

Chapter 3

Taking a Stand Against TYRANNY

Before the colonists had decided how to handle the Stamp Act, Parliament issued yet another new law in the colonies. The Quartering Act of 1765 stated that colonial legislatures were required to provide food, lodging, and supplies to English soldiers stationed in America. The people felt that this act was yet another example of taxation without representation. Once again it called for the colonists to pay for items without their consent.

Many colonists were concerned about why the British soldiers were staying in America now that the French and Indian War was over. They didn't see a need for them during a time of peace. The government, however, insisted that the soldiers would help to protect the colonists from any further trouble from the French.

The people were less than thrilled by the soldiers' presence. During the war, the colonists helped out however they could. They contributed money to the cause. Many of them also risked their lives to help

The Quartering Act demanded that colonists provide the British soldiers with lodging as well as supplies.

defend the colonies from the French. They did these things voluntarily. Now, however, the colonists didn't see providing for the British soldiers as their responsibility.

Many of the colonists were refusing to pay for the British troops' ammunition, uniforms, and other supplies. This angered General Thomas Gage, the Commander-in-Chief of Forces in British North America. He asked Parliament to force the colonists to live up to what he saw as their financial obligation.

Parliament responded by issuing the Quartering Act. This new law required the colonists to do even more for the English soldiers than they had already been doing. They were already burdened with the costs of the troops' food, firewood, and even beer. Now they also had to provide them with housing. Just as some people think the Stamp Act was about postage, some also misunderstand the Quartering Act. They think that

General Thomas Gage thought it was the colonists' duty to provide food, lodging, and supplies to the British soldiers. When the colonists refused, he took the matter to Parliament, asking the British government to make the colonists comply. Parliament responded by creating the Quartering Act.

soldiers took over people's homes. This wasn't the case, but they did have the right to take up residence in privately owned property.

In some areas there wasn't enough public housing for the soldiers. In these cases the Quartering Act forced owners of inns, stables, and ale houses to provide lodging for the troops. The owners of these businesses were not paid for this use. Eventually, barns and empty houses were also added to the list of places the soldiers could use free of charge without the consent of owners.

King George III

As Parliament passed more and more new laws in the colonies, the colonists were becoming more and more upset. One of the most basic principles of English law was that no person should be taxed without having a voice in government. The colonists were beginning to see King George III as a tyrant.

As soon as the war had ended, New York passed a bill stating that the colony would provide for the soldiers. But since New York had the busiest harbor in America, more troops came to this colony than any other. Soon, the colony became flooded with troops. This left New York with the heaviest burden from the Quartering Act.

In January of 1766, fifteen hundred more soldiers arrived in New York.[1] By this time, New Yorkers were fed up with being forced to support large numbers of English troops. The New York Assembly refused to continue to meet the terms of the Quartering Act. The soldiers were forced to stay on their ships, but the dispute raged on. One clash over the issue became so violent, in fact, that a colonist was killed.

Parliament responded to New York's refusal by passing yet another law the following year. This one was called the New York Restraining Act. It removed the New York governor from power and prevented the legislature from convening until the colony agreed to pay for all the troops' needs. Even this, however, didn't settle the problem. New York decided to challenge Parliament with an extreme measure of its own. The merchants of the colony issued a boycott of all British goods.

In addition to the boycott, New York refused to let Parliament control the activities of the colony's legislature. The Assembly issued a statement saying that Parliament had no right to stop the lawmaking group from meeting. Eventually, the legislature passed a new bill stating that the colony would pay part of the soldiers' expenses. Nowhere in the bill, however, did the Assembly even mention the Quartering Act. The colony didn't mind providing the soldiers with some supplies, but they couldn't provide all of them. Just as importantly, they didn't like being told that they *had* to do it.

Massachusetts was one of the colonies that had very little public housing for the soldiers. The only barracks it could offer the troops was on Castle Island in Boston Harbor. Living on the island made the soldiers' job more difficult. They couldn't very well control the rebellious colonists from so far away. The troops decided to commandeer Boston Common instead. They pitched their tents in the center of Boston. Many of them stayed there for several years.[2]

Being closer to the colonists didn't make things easier for anyone. All the soldiers did by forcing themselves on the town was anger the colonists. The number of squabbles between the British troops and the colonists rose quickly during this time. The intensity of these exchanges also increased. The colonists' resentment towards England was growing as well. If something didn't change soon, a much larger conflict would inevitably rise.

The Real Reason for the Troops

Keeping large numbers of British troops in America was a way for England to keep the colonists under its control. The colonists seemed to be rebelling against British rule more and more, and these officers could stop these small uprisings. In some cases, the soldiers' presence could even prevent rebellions from happening. The English officers were also used to collecting taxes and enforcing new laws.

Another reason England hadn't brought the British officers home was due to finances. England was already suffering financially from the war, and providing pensions to a large number of troops would make things even tougher.[3] Just as Parliament was taxing the colonists, the government was also taxing the people back home. It was much easier to keep the soldiers in America where the colonists were already taking care of them.

England also worried that removing troops from the colonies would weaken its relationships with the country's wealthiest families. It had become a tradition for England to offer the sons of wealthy British families high-ranking positions in the British military. Doing so helped strengthen the loyalties of these families to the British government. Parliament worried about what would happen to this financial relationship if there were no positions to give these young men.

British Redcoat
soldier

Chapter 4

Rising
TENSIONS

The colonists were holding firm in their belief that Parliament did not have the right to tax them without their consent. One of the most vocal opponents of England's taxes on the colonies was Benjamin Franklin. On February 13, 1766, Franklin appeared before the House of Commons to discuss the matter. He spoke for more than four hours, answering 174 questions.[1]

Franklin spoke about the importance of giving the colonists the same rights that English citizens possessed. He explained that doing so would help ensure peace between England and its North American colonies. He specifically urged Parliament to repeal the Stamp Act, which had caused much resentment from the colonists.

A skilled speaker, Franklin made some excellent points. He did such a good job stating the colonists' case that Parliament agreed to repeal the Stamp Act. This was made official in March of 1766. Try as he may, though, Franklin could not convince the

Among the colonists who opposed the Stamp Act and additional taxation, was Benjamin Franklin. He appeared before the House of Commons in 1766, speaking for more than four hours about the matter.

members of Parliament that the colonists deserved all the same rights as the citizens of England.

They followed up the repeal of the Stamp Act with the Declaratory Act. Although it didn't impose any new taxes, this new law was much harsher than the Stamp Act had been. It declared that England had full authority to make laws for the colonists—"in all cases whatsoever."[2]

This move put an even greater strain on the relationship between the colonists and England. Most of the colonists accepted the fact that Parliament had the right to make laws for the colonies. They still saw a big difference between taxation and other legislation, however. Parliament refused to draw a line between the two types of laws. The British government was declaring absolute power over the American colonies.

Tensions in the colonies were already running high when Parliament issued the Townshend Acts the following year. These new laws expanded the list of taxable goods to include glass, lead, oil, paint, paper, and tea. Altogether, the new taxes on these items alone would raise more than 40,000 pounds each year for England.[3]

Parliament planned to use the money raised by the Townshend Acts to pay the salaries of the colonial governors. Although this may sound like a simple financial matter, the purpose was actually much more complicated. Before the Townshend Acts, each governor was paid by his individual colony's legislature. If the assembly wasn't pleased with the governor's performance, it could withhold his salary. Parliament knew that governors would have more freedom to disagree with their colonial legislatures if they didn't depend on them to be paid. The British government hoped this change would work in its own favor.

In addition to these changes, the Townshend Acts also set up a board of customs commissioners. These British employees were sent to the colonial waterfronts to make sure that the colonists were following the new tax laws. The customs officials received a bonus for each convicted smuggler they caught. As with the Sugar Act and the Stamp Act, violators would be sent to Nova Scotia for a trial before a judge. Any colonists caught smuggling would almost certainly be found guilty.

The colonists were outraged by the Townshend Acts. They decided to rebel against the law by making more organized boycotts of British goods. They drew up non-importation agreements. These written promises not to buy items from England had a damaging effect on British merchants.

Of course, not everyone stopped buying British goods. Some people continued to buy imported items, yet these people were often harassed by colonists who supported the boycotts. The colonists who most strongly opposed the Townshend Acts also harassed customs officials who collected the taxes. Parliament soon reacted by sending more British troops to America. Again, instead of solving the problem, this only angered the colonists further.

It wasn't just individuals who rebelled against the Townshend Acts. The colonial assemblies also took action against the new law. In 1768, Samuel Adams, a member of the Massachusetts legislature, penned a letter about the matter to all the colonies. In it he asked them to unite with Massachusetts in fighting the new taxes. When Parliament learned

Samuel Adams reached out to the British colonies to fight the new taxes that Parliament was creating. The British government was so upset by the letter he wrote that it threatened to remove the Massachusetts legislature from power.

of the letter, it threatened the assembly. If the legislature didn't repeal the letter, Parliament would remove the assembly from power. By a vote of 92 to 17, the legislature refused to repeal the document.[4]

Not only did Massachusetts refuse Parliament's order, but several other colonies joined the assembly in their decision to fight the Townshend Acts. These colonies included New Jersey, New York, and Rhode Island. Parliament followed through on its threat by dissolving the legislature. Still, the resistance to the act continued.

By 1769, British merchants had suffered great financial losses due to non-importation. These sellers pleaded with Parliament to work with the colonists. While Parliament was considering its next move, tensions continued to run high on the other side of the Atlantic Ocean.

On March 5, 1770, the hostilities between the soldiers and the colonists exploded—literally. British troops in Boston responded to ongoing harassment from the colonists by firing shots into a rioting crowd. Three men were killed instantly, and two more died later of their wounds. A British captain named Thomas Preston and his men were charged with murder as a result of this brutal day, known forevermore in history books as the Boston Massacre.

Parliament removed troops from the area immediately in hopes of easing the colonists' fears and preventing further violence. The local courts also did their part to lower anxiety over the incident. They postponed the trials of the soldiers by several months. Still, the events drew an outpouring of support for the resistance against England. Up until this point, many people were on the fence over whether to rebel against English rule. Now most of these colonists had made up their minds to side with the Patriots, as the rebels were now being called.

Shortly after the violence in Boston, Parliament decided to offer the colonists a compromise on the Townshend Acts. In April, the government issued a partial repeal of these new laws. It removed taxes on all imported goods except for one. To prevent itself from appearing too weak, Parliament decided to keep the tax on tea. This one decision would have a bigger effect on England and its colonies than perhaps any other since the French and Indian War.

Facts About the Boston Massacre

- The events of March 5, 1770, would come to be known by several names in the coming years. Today, nearly everyone refers to the event as the Boston Massacre. The first popular name for the incident was the Bloody Massacre in King Street. By the early 1800s, people often called it the State Street Massacre.
- Among the five men who died in the Boston Massacre was a former slave named Crispus Attucks. He was the first African American to die as a result of the conflict between England and the American colonies. Many people consider him the first African American casualty of the American Revolution.
- A popular story states that Captain John Goldfinch shot into the crowd because a colonist was harassing him about an unpaid bill to his wigmaker. It is, in fact, true that Goldfinch had an overdue bill to his wigmaker, but it has been proven that he settled the debt the day before the Boston Massacre.
- Some people think that the Boston Massacre marked the beginning of the American Revolution, but that isn't accurate. Although the incident was among the reasons the colonists went to war with England, many other events occurred before war was officially declared.

The Boston Massacre took place March 5, 1770. Crispus Attucks was one of five men killed in the incident.

Chapter 5

From Rebellion to
REVOLUTION

British merchants were extremely pleased with the partial repeal of the Townshend Acts. They hoped the change would return the business they had lost as a result of non-importation in the colonies. With nearly all the taxes removed, colonists would have no reason to keep the non-importation agreements in place.

Merchants in the colonies had very different feelings on the matter. When the colonists were refusing to buy goods from English sellers, these customers spent their money locally. In this way, the Townshend Acts had been very profitable for businesses in America. For this reason, they wanted the non-importation agreements to stay in effect. Most of them urged the colonists to continue the boycott of all British goods until the tax on tea was lifted.

The item that Parliament chose to maintain the tax on was also no small matter. Tea was a very popular drink in the middle of the 18th century, both in England and America. The colonists drank about

During the Boston Tea Party, enraged colonists dumped more than $1 million worth of tea into Boston Harbor.

1.2 million pounds of tea each year.[1] England was sure that the colonists wouldn't simply stop buying it.

The colonists did not stop drinking tea, but they did stop buying it from England. For many years, a large number of merchants in the colonies had been smuggling tea into America from Holland. Parliament was aware of the smuggling, but they couldn't do much to stop it. And some colonists who didn't want to break the law did buy English tea.

No matter how much they loved their tea, colonists who felt most strongly about unjust taxes remained strong. To them the issue wasn't about the specific goods, or even the tax, but rather the principle. *No taxation without representation!* The fact of the matter was that England was still insisting on charging the colonists taxes without their consent.

Parliament tried to solve two problems at once when it passed the Tea Act of 1773 on May 10, 1773. Its first concern was the East India Company, which was on the brink of bankruptcy. Under the new plan, the East India Company would ship tea directly to the colonies at a very reasonable price. Loyalist merchants in the colonies would then sell this tea to the rest of the colonists. These merchants would also be the only people allowed to sell the tea.

Parliament hoped that its second reason for passing the Tea Act was less obvious. Even though the price of tea was extremely low, England was still taxing the import. If the colonists agreed to buy the tea, they would be accepting England's right to tax them. Clever colonists weren't fooled by this plan. The Patriots urged the American tea merchants not to agree to this arrangement.

Patriots in New York City and Philadelphia, Pennsylvania, managed to convince the Loyalists to refuse to sell the East India Company tea. But the merchants in Boston would not listen. A ship called the *Dartmouth* was due to arrive in the colonies that November. The tea on the ship, by today's value, would be worth about $1 million.[2]

The *Dartmouth* arrived in Boston Harbor on November 28, 1773. The taxes on the tea were due as soon as the shipment was unloaded. If the

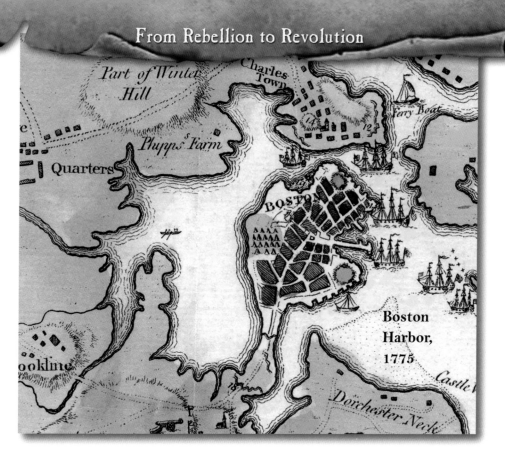

Part of Winter Hill

Charles Town

Ferry Boat

Phipps Farm

Quarters

BOSTON

Boston Harbor, 1775

ookline

Castle

Dorchester Neck

colonists didn't pay the taxes within 20 days, English soldiers would seize the cargo.

Patriots posted notices all over town:

"Friends! Brethren! Countrymen!—That worst of plagues, the detested tea, shipped for this port by the East India Company, is now arrived in the harbor; the hour of destruction, or manly opposition to the machinations of tyranny, stares you in the face. Every friend to his country, to himself and to posterity, is now called upon to meet at Faneuil Hall, at nine o'clock THIS DAY (at which time the bells will ring), to make united and successful resistance to this last, worst, and most destructive measure of administration."[3]

An enormous crowd of colonists assembled at Faneuil Hall. So many people showed up that the hall could not contain them all. The group decided to move the proceedings to the Old South Meeting House. There, they decided to work together to prevent the tea from being unloaded. If the shipment could not be delivered, no taxes could be charged. They informed the *Dartmouth's* captain that the ship should be

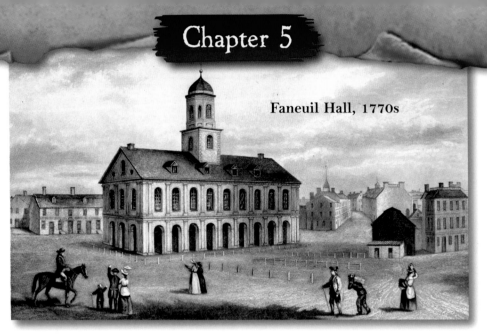

Faneuil Hall, 1770s

moored at Griffin's Wharf. They made it very clear that under no circumstance was the cargo to be unloaded.

Two more ships carrying tea were expected to enter the harbor by the end of the day. They too would be instructed to moor alongside the *Dartmouth*. The group appointed 20 colonists to stand guard. Their only job was to make sure that no tea was unloaded. Other colonists took on the job of carrying the news to neighboring towns. If the ships tried to unload the tea, the Patriots would need all the help they could get in preventing it from happening.

The ships sat in the harbor as the local governments tried to resolve the issue. The men on the ships had unloaded all their cargo except for the tea, and they wanted to return home. Governor Thomas Hutchinson, however, did not want the vessels to leave until the tea had also been delivered to the merchants. He ordered British forces to place two ships in the entrance to the harbor to prevent the ships from leaving. Neither side was backing down.

December 16 was the planned deadline for the taxes on the *Dartmouth's* tea shipment. On this day, an even larger group of colonists gathered at the Old South Meeting House to discuss the matter. The meeting began with 2,000 men in attendance and quickly grew to more than 7,000.[4] It was the largest crowd ever assembled in the town of

Boston. The men spilled from the large building out into the streets. One of the men was John Hancock, a well-known Patriot merchant.

When it became obvious that neither side was going to give in, a voice in the crowd offered up an Indian-like war-whoop. The sound was immediately met by similar battle cries. Another Patriot shouted, "Boston Harbor a teapot tonight! Hurrah for Griffin's Wharf!" The crowd responded by setting forth to the wharf at once. Leading the march was a group of colonists who had disguised themselves as Indians.

The Loyalists would not allow the ships to leave the harbor, so the Patriots decided to unload the shipments themselves—right into Boston Harbor. More than 60 men boarded the vessels and immediately began throwing the chests of tea overboard. By the time they were done, the Patriots had dumped 342 chests of tea into the water. The events of this evening would later be referred to as the Boston Tea Party.

The Boston Tea Party took place on a British ship called the *Dartmouth* on December 16, 1773. During the protest, the enraged colonists tossed 342 chests of tea into the water. Not only would they not pay taxes on the tea, but England would not be able to sell it to anyone else.

It took some time for the news of the Boston Tea Party to reach England. King George III and Parliament knew about the incident by January 1774, but it was not made public until March of that year. The king wanted to make sure that he had enough evidence before taking any action. After receiving letters from Hutchinson and other Loyalist governors, a British admiral, and numerous tea merchants, the king asked Parliament to deal with the matter. He wanted the rebellion in the colonies to be stopped once and for all.

The British government decided that the colonists should be punished for their flagrant disrespect. Since Parliament saw the Bostonians as the ringleaders of the rebellion, it decided to focus the punishment on them. The government would shut down Boston Harbor until the Bostonians agreed to submit to England's full authority over their colony. Once this happened, the king would then re-open the port as he saw fit.

Edmund Burke

A small number of Parliament members opposed the idea of closing the harbor. One of them, a man named Edmund Burke, tried to convince the rest that they were making a big mistake. "You wish to condemn the accused without a hearing," he told them; "to punish indiscriminately the innocent with the guilty! You will thus irrevocably alienate the hearts of the colonists from the mother country."[5]

Burke went on to explain that Boston was not the only area in the colonies that was rebelling. He thought that the king and Parliament should consider allowing the colonists to govern themselves. He pointed out that England might not have the necessary number of troops and ships to enforce the colonies' submission. What if all of the colonies came together to fight as one against England?

Once again, the majority of Parliament refused to consider any option but complete and utter control over the American colonies. England would follow through with the original plan to suppress the Bostonians, and any other colonists who acted out against their mother country. To help accomplish this goal, Parliament looked to its British troops that were already stationed in the colonies.

General Gage concocted a secret plan. He and his troops would enter the town of Lexington in the Massachusetts colony. There they hoped to capture John Hancock and Samuel Adams, two men who they believed were leading the rebellions. They then planned to head to Concord to seize a large amount of gunpowder from the rebels. Before they could attack, however, American spies learned of Gage's plan.

The only thing the Patriots didn't know was whether the British troops would be coming by land or by sea. To help spread the word once they found out, they created their own plan. Lanterns would be placed in the tower of the Old North Church. A single lantern would alert the town of Boston to a land attack, and two would mean the troops were arriving by sea.

On the night of April 18, 1775, the signal appeared. As soon as the two lights appeared above the town, a group of riders mounted their horses. Their job was to announce the attack to the colonists in outlying areas. Colonial militias responded immediately. These men were often called minutemen because of the fact that they could be ready to fight in a minute's notice.

No one knows for sure whether the British or the Patriots fired the first shot of the American Revolution. Regardless of the answer, that "shot heard round the world" changed the futures of both England and what would soon be the United States of America.

Soon, hundreds of British soldiers had arrived on the Lexington Green, where the colonial militias had been waiting for them. Suddenly, a shot was fired. To this day, historians still debate whether the British troops or the minutemen fired first, but one thing is certain: that single shot—often referred to as the "shot heard round the world"—marked the beginning of the American Revolution, the war that would win the colonies their independence from England.

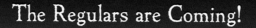

The Regulars are Coming!

Several colonists rode through the Boston countryside on the night of April 18, 1775. They included Paul Revere, William Dawes, and Samuel Prescott. Most of the accounts of that fateful night give all the credit to Revere. This is in part because of a poem written in 1860 by Henry Wadsworth Longfellow, *The Midnight Ride of Paul Revere*.

Revere and Dawes set out together to warn the colonists and alert the minutemen to the impending attack by the British troops. The men took separate routes through town. By splitting up, they helped to ensure that the message could still be spread even if one of them was captured by British soldiers.

Along their way, Revere and Dawes were met by another Patriot named Samuel Prescott. He then joined the pair in alerting the people of Boston and the surrounding towns. The plan to ride separately turned out to be a good one. A group of six British soldiers captured Revere and proceeded to question him at length. Dawes ended up losing his horse, which forced him to continue to Lexington on foot. Prescott, however, continued on to Concord to finish the job.

Often, people mistakenly think that the riders shouted the words, "The British are coming!" as they galloped through each town. In 1774, however, this message would have only confused the public. At the time, colonists still thought of themselves as British. It is much more likely that Revere, Dawes, and Prescott yelled, "The regulars are coming!" The word *regular* was a slang term for "British soldier."

1754	The French defeat Lieutenant Colonel George Washington and his army.
1755	The French defeat British Major General Edward Braddock. He and the majority of his men are killed in the battle.
1756–1763	French and Indian War
1758	Washington and his men defeat the French by capturing Fort Duquesne.
1760	King George III's reign begins.
1763	The Treaty of Paris is signed, officially ending the French and Indian War.
1764	Parliament replaces the Molasses Act with the Sugar Act and re-issues the Currency Act; James Otis writes *"The Rights of the British Colonies Asserted and Proved."*
1765	Parliament passes the Stamp Act; Thomas Whately writes *"The Regulations Lately Made Concerning the Colonies and the Taxes Imposed Upon Them Considered;"* Daniel Dulany writes *"Considerations*

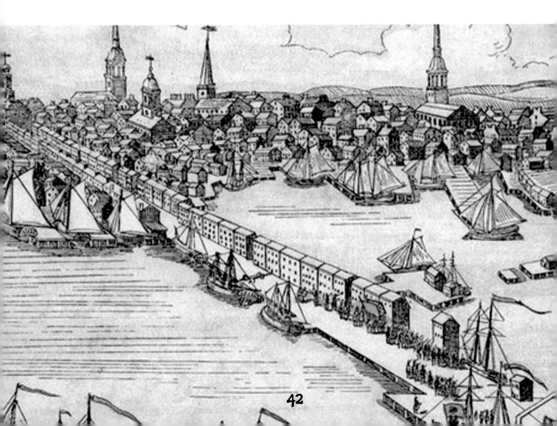

on the Propriety of Imposing Taxes in the British Colonies;" the Stamp Act Congress convenes; Parliament issues the Quartering Act.

1766   Fifteen hundred soldiers arrive in New York; the colony responds by refusing to abide by the Quartering Act; New York merchants boycott British goods; Benjamin Franklin speaks before the House of Commons; Parliament repeals the Stamp Act and issues the Declaratory Act.

1767   Parliament issues the Townshend Acts.

1768   Samuel Adams writes a letter to all the colonies, asking them to join Massachusetts in fighting new taxes. When the legislature refuses to repeal the letter, Parliament dissolves the Massachusetts Assembly.

1770   Five colonists are killed in the Boston Massacre; Parliament makes a partial appeal of the Townshend Acts.

1773   Parliament passes the Tea Act.

1774   The Boston Tea Party takes place in Boston Harbor.

1775   British troops attack the colonies in Lexington and Concord; the American Revolution begins.

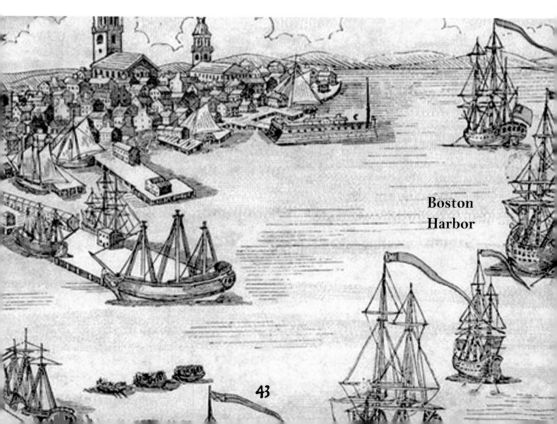

Boston
Harbor

Chapter 1. Fighting Together, Splitting Apart

1. National Park Service, The Braddock Campaign. http://www.nps.gov/fone/braddock.htm

2. Donald N. Moran, "Why George Washington?" *The Valley Newsletter,* February, March, 1996. http://www.revolutionarywararchives.org/washwhyhim.html

3. Founding.com, A Project of the Claremont Institute. http://www.founding.com/timeline/pageid.2460/default.asp

Chapter 2. Finding Allies in Each Other

1. Founding.com, A Project of the Claremont Institute. http://www.founding.com/timeline/pageid.2460/default.asp

2. Ibid.

3. Francis D. Cogliano, "Was the American Revolution Inevitable?" *BBC,* February 17, 2011. http://www.bbc.co.uk/history/british/empire_seapower/american_revolution_01.shtml

Chapter 3. Taking a Stand Against Tyranny

1. Boston Tea Party Ships and Museum. http://www.bostonteapartyship.com/the-quartering-act

2. History.com. http://www.history.com/this-day-in-history/parliament-passes-the-quartering-act

3. Laws.com. http://government-programs.laws.com/quartering-act

Chapter 4. Rising Tensions

1. Massachusetts Historical Society. http://www.masshist.org/revolution/doc-viewer.php?item_id=251

2. Constitution Society. http://www.constitution.org/bcp/decl_act.txt

3. USHistory.org. http://www.ushistory.org/declaration/related/townshend.htm

4. USHistory.org. http://www.ushistory.org/us/9d.asp

Chapter 5. From Rebellion to Revolution

1. Old South Meeting House. http://www.oldsouthMeeting House.org/osmh_123456789files/BostonTeaPartyBegan.aspx#howitbegan

2. Ibid.

3. Boston Tea Party Historical Society. http://www.boston-tea-party.org/in-depth.html

4. Ibid.

5. Ibid.

Books

Fradin, Dennis Brindell. *Let It Begin Here!: Lexington and Concord: First Battles of the American Revolution*. London: Walker Children's Paperbacks, 2009.

Freedman, Russell. *The Boston Tea Party*. New York: Holiday House, 2012.

Osborne, Mary Pope. *Revolutionary War on Wednesday*. New York: Random House for Young Readers, 2000.

Works Consulted

Allison, Robert. *The American Revolution: A Concise History*. New York: Oxford University Press, 2011.

Carp, Benjamin L. *Rebels Rising: Cities and the American Revolution*. New York: Oxford University Press, 2007.

Carr, J. Revell. *Seeds of Discontent: The Deep Roots of the American Revolution*. New York: Walker and Company, 2008.

Wood, Gordon S. *The Idea of America: Reflections on the Birth of the United States*. New York: Penguin Press, 2011.

On the Internet

American Revolution

http://www.ducksters.com/history/american_revolution.php

The American Revolutionary War

http://www.socialstudiesforkids.com/subjects/revolutionarywar.htm

American Revolution Web Project, Colonial Williamsburg

http://research.history.org/DHC/AmRev.cfm

KidsKonnect.com, American Revolution

http://www.kidskonnect.com/subjectindex/16-educational/history/251-american-revolution.html

GLOSSARY

bankruptcy (BANGK-ruhp-see)—The state of having less money than one's debt and therefore being unable to pay that debt.

commandeer (kom-uhn-DEER)—To take by force.

delegate (DEL-ih-gut)—A person who represents a larger group of people.

distillery (dih-STIL-uh-ree)—A place where liquor is made.

Loyalist (LOY-uh-list)—A person who remained loyal to England during the American Revolution.

militia (mi-LISH-uh)—A group of citizens who perform military duties in emergencies.

moor—To secure a ship to a dock.

Patriot (PAY-tree-uht)—A person who supported the colonies during the American Revolution.

pension (PEN-shuhn)—An amount of money paid to a person upon retirement.

repeal (ree-PEEL)—To formally withdraw.

smuggle (SMUHG-uhl)—To import an item illegally.

textile (TEKS-tyle)—Woven, knit, or felted cloth.

tyrant (TY-ruhnt)—A ruler who abuses his or her power.

MEET THE
AUTHOR

Tammy Gagne is a freelance writer who has authored numerous books for both adults and children. In her spare time, she enjoys visiting schools to speak to children about the writing process. Gagne resides in northern New England with her husband, son, and a menagerie of animals.